DEDICATED TO
JAY AND CHARLES LOSE,
WHO DO NOT WEAR BEARDS

AND TO
TOBARON WAXMAN,
WHO DOES

**TABLE OF CONTENTS**

1. TITLE PAGE
2. COPYRIGHT PAGE
3. DEDICATION
4. PREMISE
5. MORE ABOUT BEARDS
6. GROWN-UPS
7. WOMEN
8. LION
9. MATCHING
10. SKIRTS
11. MOUNTAIN CLIMBERS
12. NO BEARDS
13. MUSICIANS
14. LION-TAILED MACAQUE
15. WIZARDS
16. DEVOUT MEMBERS
17. DRAGONS
18. COOL CATS
19. MOUNTAIN GOATS
20. PLAYOFFS
21. LUMBERJACKS
22. DOGS
23. SURFERS
24. COMPETITION
25. SHIP CAPTAIN
26. BISON
27. SEALS
28. GNOMES
29. MEDICAL
30. FLOWER
31. MARAKOR
32. WEEVIL
33. CONCLUSION

**THIS BOOK TELLS A STORY ABOUT BEARDS. BEARDS CAN BE FACIAL HAIR ON PEOPLE. HERE ARE SOME BEARDS FOR PEOPLE.**

**BEARDS ON ANIMALS AND FLOWERS ARE DIFFERENT THAN FACIAL HAIR. THE LION, BEARDED DRAGON, AND IRIS FLOWER ALL HAVE BEARDS. YET, NONE OF THEIR BEARDS LOOK ALIKE.**

**YOU HAVE TO GROW UP TO HAVE A BEARD. MOST KIDS DON'T HAVE BEARDS.**

**WOMEN MAY OCCASIONALLY GROW BEARDS. BUT ONLY SOME WOMEN GROW THEM.**

**THE LION'S MANE IS A BEARD. IT IS BIG AND SHAGGY AND GOES ALL THE WAY AROUND THEIR HEAD.**

**SOME MEN DYE THEIR HAIR TO MATCH THEIR BEARDS. THEY MIGHT WANT THEIR BEARDS TO MATCH THEIR SHIRT TOO.**

**SOME MEN WHO WEAR BEARDS LIKE SKIRTS**

**MOUNTAIN CLIMBERS MAY HAVE BEARDS TO KEEP THEM WARMER, ESPECIALLY WHEN THEY CLIMB HIGH.**

**THERE ARE PEOPLE WHO CAN GROW BEARDS BUT DECIDE NOT TO HAVE BEARDS.**

**THE LION-TAILED MACAQUE IS CALLED BOTH THE BEARD APE AND THE WANDEROO.**

**A WIZARD'S BEARD IS EXTRA LONG BECAUSE THEY LIVE MANY MAGICAL YEARS.**

**DEVOUT MEMBERS OF SOME RELIGIONS GROW BEARDS, WHILE OTHERS IN THE SAME FAITH MAY SHAVE THEIR FACES. IT JUST DEPENDS.**

**SOME REPTILES ARE BEARDED DRAGONS. THEIR BEARD IS ON THEIR THROAT. THEY CAN CHANGE THE COLOR WHEN THEY GET MAD.**

**PEOPLE MIGHT WEAR BEARDS TO MAKE THEMSELVES LOOK COOL OR HIP.**

**A MOUNTAIN GOAT'S BEARD IS CALLED A GOATEE.**

**HOCKEY PLAYERS MAY GROW BEARDS DURING THE PLAYOFFS. IT'S CALLED A PLAYOFF BEARD AND MAKES THEM LOOK ALIKE.**

ALMOST ALL LOGGERS WEAR BEARDS. LOGGERS ARE ALSO CALLED LUMBERJACKS.

SEVERAL DOG BREEDS HAVE BEARDS, LIKE MINIATURE SCHNAUZERS, BEARDED COLLIES, AND GERMAN WIREHAIRED POINTERS.

**SOMETIMES YOU WILL SEE SURFERS WEARING LONG BEARDS TO MATCH THEIR LONG HAIR.**

A WORLD MUSTACHE AND BEARD COMPETITION GIVES PRIZES IN THE CATEGORIES OF MUSTACHE, PARTIAL, AND COMPLETE BEARD.

**LONG AGO, VIKINGS SAILED THE SEAS, AND THEY HAD BEARDS. TODAY, SHIP CAPTAINS USUALLY HAVE BEARDS LIKE THE VIKINGS DID LONG AGO.**

**BISON HAVE BEARDS AND A HUMP ON THEIR BACKS. BUFFALO DO NOT HAVE BEARDS OR HUMPS.**

**BEARDED SEALS HAVE SUPER SENSITIVE WHISKERS. THEY USE THEM FOR HUNTING AND LOCATING FOOD.**

**GNOMES ARE MYTHIC CREATURES WHO GET BEARDS WHEN THEY TURN 400 YEARS OLD. THEY LIKE TO HIDE IN FORESTS AND GARDENS.**

**BOTH DOCTORS AND NURSES SOMETIMES WEAR BEARDS. SOMETIMES THEY DO NOT. IT IS THEIR CHOICE.**

**THIS FLOWER IS A BEARDED IRIS. ITS BEARD IS THE FUZZY YELLOW PART AT THE CENTER.**

**THE MARKHOR WEARS A BEARD TO KEEP WARM. IT'S THE NATIONAL ANIMAL OF PAKISTAN, A COUNTRY WITH MANY MOUNTAINS TO CLIMB.**

**BEARDED WEEVILS LIVE IN RAINFORESTS AND HAVE LONG SNOUTS.**

**BEARDS COME IN ALL SHAPES AND SIZES--LIKE PEOPLE, ANIMALS, FLOWERS, AND INSECTS.**

www.ingramcontent.com/pod-product-compliance
Lightning Source LLC
Chambersburg PA
CBHW041746040426
42444CB00004B/185